THE MARRIAGE MANUAL

BJ & LAURIE WOODARD

© Copyright 2009 BJ & Laurie Woodard

True Love Publishing

www.themarriagemanual.com

All rights reserved. No part of this publication may be reproduced or transmitted in any form or by any means, electronic, mechanical, photocopy or otherwise or stored on any retrieval system of any nature without prior written permission of the copyright holder.

DISCLAIMER

Every effort has been made to ensure the information in this publication is accurate and correct. BJ & Laurie Woodard, their employees and agents do not accept any responsibility or liability, whatsoever, for any error, omission, interpretation or opinion which may be present, however it occurred, nor for the consequences of any decision based on the information supplied in this publication. BJ & Laurie Woodard, their employees and agents expressly disclaim all liability to any person relying on the whole or any part of this publication.

ISBN: 978-0-578-02265-9

To our daughter Zoe

"To love one's self is the beginning
of a life long romance"

—Oscar Wilde

CONTENTS

Part 1
"It Is All About Me!
How To Make It Stay That Way."
Answers for Her
13

Part 2
"How To Get Lucky
Over and Over and Over"
Answers for Him
41

Acknowledgments

We sincerely thank all the men and women who generously shared their stories. Their tales of need and longing encouraged us to write this book. We hope it will inspire all who wish to change the course of their marriage and develop the greatest feeling on Earth, love.

We relied on many people along the way to help us make this the best book possible. Thanks to everyone who offered us guidance, ideas, suggestions and criticism.

Finally, thanks to our readers! Thank you for taking an interest in making your marriage better. Our mission is for you to recognize that you are LOVABLE. The love you deserve is achievable.

INTRODUCTION

Dear Reader,

Congratulations! If you are married, you have taken an oath before your God, family and friends to honor, cherish, and love each other until you die. If not, you have taken the first step to creating a loving relationship with your potential spouse.

Many people have an ideal vision of marriage, but the reality is different. The National Center for Health Statistics reported nearly one out of two marriages ends in divorce. How can you be sure you are in the 50% that remains married?

"The same question occurred to me. After an unfortunate divorce, I met my current husband. He seemed too good to be true and I wanted to make sure I was not a statistic."

—Laurie Woodard

In this new marriage, we were happy most of the time. We often thought we listened to each other. However, we did not always hear what the other person was saying. We wanted to find out if other couples experienced this difficulty. As a result, we spent three years surveying 500 married couples.

Our survey found couples were not able to communicate their wishes effectively. Each person had essential needs that went unmet.

Unfulfilled needs promote negative behavior. The longer a desire remains unanswered, the worse we feel. Think about the last time your need was not met. How did it affect you?

The goal of this book is to help you recognize what your partner needs most from you. This simple guide clearly identifies the most common needs men and women have.

Read the manual and consider the needs of your spouse. You will learn what is missing from your relationship. If you find and meet your partner's needs, you will have a happy and loving marriage.

Anyone can apply the included examples, information and checklists. The manual is easy to use and increases communication and intimacy!

The advice works quickly. Your marriage will improve instantly, regardless of the circumstances! The Marriage Manual is for anyone who wants a marriage full of joy.

Best of all, The Marriage Manual is not complicated. It is the perfect solution to **prevent bad habits** that lead to divorce.

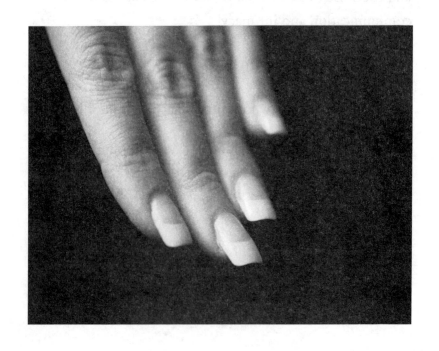

PART I

"It Is All About Me! How To Make It Stay That Way."

Answers For Her

Dear (wife) _____,

Appreciate and accept me
for the way I am.

Your caring reactions to the things I do
make me a loving man.

Excuse my imperfections;
trust I know right from wrong.

Don't misinterpret my silence
and we will get along.

I Love You_____

INTRODUCTION

A man will fall in love with a woman who makes him feel special, important, powerful, and alive. **She makes him feel good!** What attracts a man beyond chemistry, is a woman who is positive, enthusiastic, and adventurous. Reinforce that attraction by letting your man know he can be himself without judgment or criticism.

After taking wedding vows, even if he was reluctant to do so, something within him transforms. His heart now belongs to you and it will be rare if he leaves. You have the power to make your marriage everything that you want it to be.

Listed on the following pages are the ways your man needs to be "needed" by you.

If you *satisfy* his needs, the result is a devoted and loving man who **wants** to please you. He genuinely enjoys being around you. There is no need for tricks or manipulation to make your marriage work. When you learn to use this information properly, your husband cannot help himself from falling in love with you again!

COMMUNICATING WITH YOUR MAN

Happy couples share thoughts, feelings, hopes, dreams, hurt, anger and longing. They talk and listen to each other. As a result, these couples share a bond. They are each other's best friend.

LISTENING TO YOUR MAN

Practice listening and asking questions. One great way to do this is to "parrot" back what he said to you. Listen to what he said and repeat what you heard. This will prove to him that you are listening. It will also give him the opportunity to clarify anything that is unclear. If your husband does not feel like you understand what he is saying he will not want to talk to you.

TALKING TO YOUR MAN

Men love women who have the strength and confidence to communicate their wishes. If you want your husband to hear what you have to say, learn how to speak **Man**!

How to speak Man

If you ask your husband a question, make sure it is a question and not you making a statement. *Listen* to his answer. If you do not like the answer, wait until he is gone before you ask someone else the same question!

If you have forgotten what he told you the first time, ask him again. Let him know why you are asking again. He may feel like you have not listened to him.

Think about when you were dating and how attentive you were to his every word! He loved the attention even if you did not care about what he was saying. There is nothing sexier to him than having you listen to him, especially, when you are easily persuaded or liable to give in to temptation.

Do not be a nag. Asking your husband to do the same thing more than two times is nagging. If what you are asking for is time sensitive, let him know **when** you need it done. Ask him when he plans to do it. If it is still not done **do not** ask again. He may not want to do it. Make other arrangements!

Watch the **tone** of your voice. Men react to how you speak and not necessarily what you say. Men feel women can be too loud and irrational in their delivery. This is not the most effective way to communicate with your husband!

When a woman accuses, acts distrustful or insecure, nags, or belittles, what men hear is a bunch of static...like a bad radio station!

Sharing your feelings

Women mistakenly assume men need to talk and therefore should. Most men need a *reason* to talk. Men do not talk just for the sake of talking. They learned thousands of years ago to communicate without using words to achieve common goals. Watch men hunting or playing a team sport and you will understand what I mean! Words are for women!

Women want to talk about their feelings with someone. Men want to be alone to work out their feelings. They do not want to cozy up on the couch for an extended conversation. Men deal with stress by minimizing. Phrases such as, "I am fine" or "It's no big deal" are common responses. Your husband needs to feel strong enough to overcome any pain or difficulty.

To begin a discussion with your husband you need to be the first one to share. Immediately thank him for listening. He will feel valued and motivated to talk. This is **powerful** and works all the time with any male! Try talking for about a paragraph. Then stop and simply say, "Thank you for listening to me".

If you start talking and get any resistance, stop! He does **not** want to hear you. You will know when it is the right time.

THE MARRIAGE MANUAL

Men do **not** understand how women *feel.* If you want your husband to understand your emotions, relate them to an experience when *he* felt similarly. Create a story he can identify with. Let him talk about how he felt. This will create an opportunity to share and communicate.

If you are worried about how to start the conversation, try the following question.

- "Do you remember how you felt before your last salary review?"

Ask him how he felt and let him talk about it. He may talk about how nervous he felt before the meeting. Explain to him that you are nervous and worried about a situation the same way he was before his review. This way he can relate his emotion to your emotion.

If you act negatively, your husband will have nothing positive to say. Remember, he does not have the need to talk! Examples of behavior that kill conversation:

- Blaming him for something

- Complaining about yourself or worse, about him

- Demanding he talks (watch as his mind goes blank!)

- Interrogating him

APPRECIATE WHO HE IS

To appreciate means to raise value. If you value him, he will strive to be his best. The success of your marriage depends on sharing your feelings in a loving and respectful way. Focus on what you **love most** about him to keep your relationship positive. What you believe your husband is, he will become!

CHANGING YOUR MAN

Most people are afraid of change and resist it as a result. Remember a time when you were talking about something new to a friend. Your friend might have been skeptical about this new idea. Even if you felt the idea was valuable, your friend may have decided to do nothing.

Your man is the same. When you try to force him to change, resistance occurs. It does not matter if the change is an improvement or not. Using guilt or abuse will not encourage him to change. **Respect** for a man is the same as **love** is to a woman.

Do not concentrate on trying to change your husband. Men realize marriage is life altering. They care about their wives enough to adjust their behavior. They will change, once they feel accepted.

What to Avoid

Do not tell him what to do. He will resist any sentence starting with, "you should" or "you need to". Examples include:

- "You should slow down. You are making me nervous."

- "You need to help me with the laundry."

Instead, start with "Would you". Do not forget to add **please** and **thank** you!

Do not offer unsolicited advice in the form of your opinion. This sabotages trust. Your man may feel like you are trying to *control* him. When he wants your idea, he will ask. If he does, be honest and helpful.

Your husband takes pride in doing tasks on his own. He may feel weak or inept if you try to help. He will ask for help if needed.

Do not speak for him. If someone asks your husband a question, let him answer.

Do not pick out his clothing unless asked. You are not his mother.

APPRECIATE WHAT HE DOES FOR YOU

Men *want* to please and *need* **praise** from you. When you show gratitude, he will want to do more for you. Simply saying "**Thank you** for helping me" can reap huge rewards and better communication!

HOW TO ASK FOR HELP

Remember a man typically will not ask for help. Asking if you need help may not occur to him.

When you need help *ask for what you want in a clear and direct way*. Mention when you would like it finished. Leave details out unless asked.

If you feel overwhelmed with work and want help, do not tell off your husband! He will not respond to you in a helpful way. Your husband may help you, but any support will not come quickly or easily.

Instead, before you ask for help make a list. Write down all the tasks you want to do. Circle the items on the list you do not want to do. Show your husband the list and explain the tasks you want to do today. Ask for his help with the circled tasks. Explain that you will be doing everything else on the list.

Explaining and showing the list allows him to see you are working and he will feel obliged to help. Finally, do not assume that just because you want help he will do it. Ask him specifically what he has time and ability to do. Ask for his thoughts about the list. You may find your talk makes the work easier by removing or consolidating certain tasks. Your husband will be much more willing to help, you will not feel overwhelmed, and both of you will have more free time to spend together!

Always begin questions with "would you". Do **not** ask using *can* or *could*. He will ponder whether he can or could. If it is important, leave no time to ponder! Do not forget to say *please* and *thank you*!

EXAMPLES:

- "Would you please pick up the laundry from the dry cleaners by 5 PM today? Thank you!"

- "Would you please go to the store for me? We are out of milk. I need it within the hour. Thank you!"

If he forgets to pick up something at the store, do not get upset. Instead, calmly ask him to return and give him a big hug. He will smile all the way!

When your man does something for you show your appreciation! Spend a few seconds thinking of a sincere *thank you*. Talk about how you feel. Tell him specifically what he has done for you to make life better or save time. Thank him with a smile and he will smile back!

APPRECIATE WHAT HE DOES FOR A LIVING

A man feels his role in a marriage is to earn a living. You want his attention. He needs your encouragement. Men do not understand that a paycheck and a bouquet of flowers have the same meaning to you!

Your husband may feel you do not care about what he does. You may be too involved with your own life, children, household or career.

Work is a huge part of a man's identity. Your husband works on his goals and needs to feel a sense of accomplishment. It is important you take an active interest in his work no matter what he does. He needs to feel support from you.

Stress is part of life and your husband feels it at work. When he comes home, let him relax. He may want to be alone, kick back and visit his cave. If he needs space, give him some. When he has had a chance to recharge, he will be all yours!

Ideas to help you start

- Ask him about his day and listen. Ask him questions if you do not understand.

- Read a book or article about his line of work.

- Surprise him with your knowledge of his career or business in front of his friends or colleagues.

- Celebrate his success.

SHARE HIS SPORT OR HOBBY

(This is optional only if you want to spend more time with him)

Everyone is busy. Couples do not spend much time together between work, social duties, and family responsibilities. If you want more "hubby" time, make the time about *him*, not you. Trust me, he would be thrilled to have you on his team!

FOOD FOR THOUGHT

- Embrace one of his interests.

- Learn his sport or his workout routine.

- Read current events and talk about them with him.

- Go to a sporting event.

- Suggest that you go to an electronics store *together*!

If your man needs time alone, do not feel hurt; it is **not** personal. Everyone has a need to be alone some of the time. Once he has time to reflect and recharge he will be more attentive and engaging.

SHOW HIM YOUR DEVOTION

A man wants a wife who is honest and trustworthy. He wants to know without doubt that he is the only one for you.

When you are in public together and see an attractive man, your husband can sense it! Squeeze your husband's arm and say, "I love you".

Another way to show devotion is to give him a compliment. Make a compliment about him in front of other people. Just like you want, remember? Give him a compliment about his appearance, cooking, performance in bed or almost anything!

EXAMPLE:

- "My husband cooked the best meal for me last night and even cleaned up!"

Spend time with him doing what **he** wants to do. Watch a TV show or movie of his choice. Let him pick the restaurant.

If your husband tells you he wants to do something pay attention! If it is important enough for him to share, you must listen. Do not think or comment about what you would rather do. This is not a time to be selfish. Be like

Nike and just "do it"! Do it because he asked and because you love him.

Do not confuse devotion with "doing a lot of things for him". If you are always giving, he may feel like a contestant in a giving competition! He wants you to compliment him not compete with him.

If you are in a bad mood let him know *at once* it is not *his* fault! If you are upset with him, try to express it quietly. Treat him as you would a friend. You would never "go off" on a good friend!

Men can handle conflict, but **no one likes to argue.** Neither side feels the other has heard them. If you do not raise your voice or use biting comments, **it will mean more to him than all the sweet words in the world!** He will feel respected and will hear you.

FIX YOURSELF UP FOR HIM

Think about when you were dating. You planned the outfits and styled your hair. You exercised and controlled your weight. Remember how good you felt!

If you want a "WOW" from him, put on a fashion show! Dressing up and asking what he likes is the fastest way to compliments. The more attractive you look, the better you feel. The better you feel, the more he will want to show you off!

If you really want him to notice change, go to the bank and take out a stack of small dollar bills. Put them in front of him and tell him this is what you spend to be beautiful for him. He will notice and **watch** you closely!

SEX

Warning: A sexless marriage is not OK!

Men like their wives to begin romance. They like when women think about sex and plan for it. The interest in sex with him is most important. Active sexual communication makes a happy hubby.

Women become excited and stimulated with words. Think about how happy you were the last time you got a poem or your husband *said* something nice to you.

What men **see** make them eager. Remember a time when your husband watched sports. When his team scored, was he wound up?

To excite your man dress up for him! Wear sexy lingerie, a nurse uniform or cheerleader outfit. Even one of his old T-shirts will do (but no stains please!). If you are big or small, he will look... you have the power to make his evening!

Men think about sex constantly. Do not disappoint him! Make a sexual gesture toward him. Give him a light massage or grab him when least expected. Everyday let him know you could ravish his body. Show him how attracted you are to him.

Show him how **self-confident you are** with your body. Sex appeal is 50% what you've got and 50% what he thinks you have. *If you think* you're sexy so will he, guaranteed!

Your husband gets great pleasure by satisfying you sexually. He loves conquest and the thrill of victory. A man never knows by looking how aroused you are. If you are about to climax, let him know!

Learn how to become an expert at giving oral sex. Do it often and enjoy doing it. He will not hold it against you if you do not swallow. The best time to do it is while he is breathing (hah ha!).

We are sorry if we have offended anyone. This has been a subject of great debate. We decided to leave it here because we are talking about him. This is one of his greatest pleasures. If he is satisfied, pleasing you will come automatically!

Give him a certificate for one night when you will lock the bedroom door and take over. Do not be afraid to let yourself go in front of your husband! The more adventurous you want to be the better. He will love it!

After childbirth, some women lose their sex drive. If this happens, your husband may feel neglected. He can be jealous of the attention you give to your child. He will not tell you this. **Don't** leave him out. He is your biggest baby of all!

DEALING WITH YOUR MAN

These are the ways in which your husband will best *receive and return your love*. He will have different needs at different times. Ignoring pain or unhappiness is one way men cope with stress. That is why, if there are problems, women will seek help first. Do not ignore your man or he will ignore you. If you do, he will shut you out of his heart forever. If your husband feels you understand him, his heart will be open to you.

If you follow this program, it will work like magic!

CHECKLIST

WHAT HAVE YOU DONE
FOR YOUR MARRIAGE TODAY?

- Have you told him how happy he makes you or how much you love him?

- Have you had a positive conversation with him?

- Have you asked him to do something for you and thanked him sincerely for doing it?

- Have you asked how his day was and shown interest in it?

- Have you fixed yourself up with him in mind?

- Have you started or talked about sex with him?

PART 2

"HOW TO GET LUCKY OVER AND OVER AND OVER"

ANSWERS FOR HIM

Dear (husband) _____,

You may never really understand me
please pretend to try.

Do not fix, change or alter
my needs that apply.

Practice them daily
like brushing your teeth.

Watch me light up
as your little bride to be.

I Love You_____

INTRODUCTION

I recently had a conversation with a man who was celebrating his 50th wedding anniversary. Married couples today rarely reach this milestone. When I asked him how he managed to do this, he simply replied, "My wife is always RIGHT, even when she is wrong!"

Your wife fell in love with you because of the way you made her **feel**. You showed her how beautiful, sexy, capable, intelligent and needed she was. This is *why* she married you!

Women craved attention from their fathers before marrying you. The need for attention still exists. THE ATTENTION YOU GIVE YOUR WIFE IS HER FOOD!

The following pages detail her "attention menu". The menu shows different kinds of food she needs and wants from you. Your wife likes them all but prefers some foods to others.

Do not be afraid to *ask* her what they are! This simple step will yield big results. Throw in surprises, but do not forget to feed her. Dish out her favorite foods and you will have everything you want!

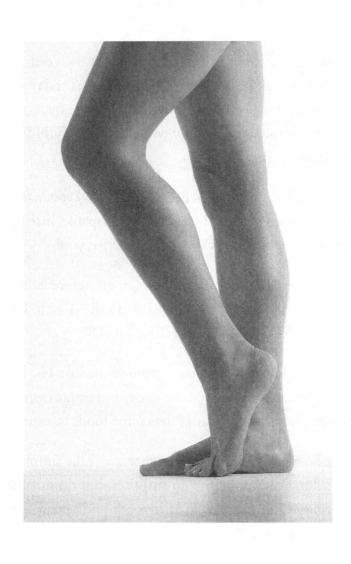

HER ATTENTION MENU

SEX

(Her "I feel desirable" food)

Warning: A sexless marriage is not OK!

Couples who are happily in love invest energy in the sexual aspect of their marriage. They make love often and sex is important! However, for each partner, sex fills a different need.

Your wife must feel emotionally attached to you before she is ready for sex. If she feels tired, bloated, or unhappy the chances for sex are slim. Sex reinforces the emotional connection men feel but do not always express.

BEFORE HAVING SEX

Women want romance; so use your imagination. Remind your wife you can be romantic and it will lead to sex. Set a mood that tells her you care. Give her your undivided attention.

If she likes candles, light them up. Consider starting a bubble bath or playing soft music. Use everything you can to make the moment feel right.

WHEN HAVING SEX

Picture what you can do or say to give her pleasure... then do it!

Your wife will become frustrated if you do not please her sexually. Work to give her an orgasm first. It is worth the effort even though it could take longer. If you please her first, she will consider you a great lover! She will want to make love with you again.

Let her know how beautiful she is to you while making love. Use your words.

Thinking Points

Pay attention to her overlooked areas. The nape of the neck, top of her breasts or arch of the foot could be sensitive spots. Ask her **where and how** she likes to be touched.

A woman's body changes with time especially with childbirth. What felt good before may not feel good now. Ask her if the way you are touching her still feels good.

Do not get in the habit of letting your child or pet sleep in the same bed with you. Three is a crowd when it comes to cuddling.

PHYSICAL AFFECTION

(This is her "I feel worthy and loved" food)

Be affectionate with her every day. Your actions speak loudly. Everyone needs to be touched like plants need sunlight. Let her know you need her anytime.

Show her you care with a hug before you leave. Give her a kiss when you come home. Yes, even before looking at the mail, petting the dog or playing with the children! Give your wife a kiss, hug, pat, or squeeze often!

OTHER IDEAS

- Give her at least three hugs a day.

- Cuddle with her without being sexual.

- Show your feelings in public. Hold hands or put your arms around her.

- Kiss and hug in front of the kids.

DO SOMETHING AROUND THE HOUSE TO HELP HER (BEFORE SHE ASKS!)

(This is her "You are getting sex tonight or not" food.)

This is critical and directly related to sex! Men cannot believe how long women go without thinking about sex. Women on the other hand cannot believe how long men go without thinking about cleaning the house.

A woman is happier when she feels her partner helps with the housework. It does not need to be an equal workload. Your wife just has to think it is reasonable! A happier wife leads to a better sex life!

We are sure if you did all the housework, laundry, childcare, grocery shopping and cooking for a week, you would be too exhausted to think about sex. If you do not believe it, try it!

It may surprise you, to know your wife spends more time worrying about getting work done than doing it. If you can afford to, hire the cleaning out! If not, help her clean so she does not feel alone. Cleaning up after yourself says a lot to her.

DON'T FORGET TO CLEAN

- Whiskers around sink

- Urine and stains around the toilet. "Ugh! This is disgusting!"

- Dirty clothes left on the floor. "When did I become your mother?"

Guys, if your wife ever says this to you, she is not happy!

Ways you can help out

- On your way home call to see if she needs anything.

- Play with kids while she cooks.

- Clear the dishes after a meal and load the dishwasher.

- Help with the kids at bath time.

- Wash her car or change the oil.

- Fix something. It is what you do best!

GIVE HER MANY COMPLIMENTS

(This is her "I feel good about myself" food and your Laid-aid)

The better your wife feels, the more she wants to be beautiful for you. Help your wife feel positive by giving her a compliment! Confirm her feelings with kind and thoughtful words. You can never give enough compliments. Feed her this food often!

We would bet praising her was easy when you were dating. Think back to how often you admired her. This meal sealed the deal!

GIVING COMPLIMENTS

We have all heard the phrase "the truth hurts". When it comes to compliments, women do not want to hear the truth! Has she ever asked, "How do I look?" Everyone knows this is a line women use when fishing for compliments. What you may not know, is it also means you did not compliment her <u>fast</u> enough. Always think about how to flatter her! If you do not, she will notice!

BE SPECIFIC

- "I like what you did with your hair; it looks cute!"

- "What a great job you did organizing the pantry, honey!"

- "This meal is better than the one we had at [insert the name of her favorite restaurant]."

- Be generous with your words.

- "You look gorgeous; I am such a lucky guy!"

Be flirtatious and watch her light up! Compliment your wife on anything — her hair, body, clothing, jewelry, cooking or who she is to you.

Happy couples talk about what they like, enjoy and admire about each other. As a result, they feel visible, understood, and valued.

BUY HER FLOWERS OR GIFTS

(This is her "dessert" and we hope yours, too!)

Although she does not need it everyday, a healthy feeding guarantees to keep her sweet. Remember small gifts are cheaper than diamonds (which work, too!).

Gifts, big or small, show that you love her. Give gifts often for no reason other than you are thinking about her. Do not forget birthdays, anniversaries or Hallmark holidays.

Make sure you get the gift! Thinking about a gift does not cut it. A $3 greeting card is better than an excuse. Add it to your calendar or to-do list.

SOME OF MY FAVORITE GIFTS

(They could be hers too!)

- Learn her favorite flowers. Buy them fresh!

- Put some thought into a surprise date or outing.

- Dinner followed by dessert.

- Buy her favorite bottle of wine or chocolate.

- Buy something for her you know she wants but feels too guilty to ask for.

Household appliances are not acceptable as gifts (unless asked for). Even then, it never hurts to throw in some flowers!

NOT ROMANTIC BUT STILL POWERFUL

Pick something up needed at home, such as eggs, milk, or toilet paper. Earn bonus points for something you know she needs.

SAY "I LOVE YOU"

(This is her "feeling-wanted" food and needed often)

Show and say you love her daily. It does not matter how. Be creative!

Tell her with a card, e-mail, text or phone call. The more often you say it, the better you both will feel! We suggest *at least* twice a day when you leave and return home.

- You never know what can happen in a day. Call her from work to let her know you were thinking about her. Leave a love note somewhere she will find it. Make sure "I love you" are the last words you said to her.

How NOT to say "I Love You"

- "I told you I loved you on our wedding night. If anything changes I will let you know."

- Ditto

- Yeah, me too

Some men believe the hunt is over when they marry. Now, all they have to do is bring home the "bacon". Your wife values money, but how you make her **feel** is more important.

Show her you love her. Tell her you love her. Above all, make sure she feels that you love her! It is not enough for her to "know" you do. If you consistently do this, she will cater to your every need. She will not want to live without you!

SPEND QUALITY TIME COMMUNICATING

(This is her "survival" food; without it your marriage will not work)

This was the number one complaint from women we interviewed. Talking or telling her how you feel is not enough. The success of your marriage is dependent on your ability to listen lovingly and respectfully to your spouse's feelings.

If it is not a good time to listen to your wife, let her know. Suggest when a better time to concentrate on her will be. Find a time when you are ready and sit down just the two of you.

If you are not sure about how to listen to your wife, try asking a question about her. Questions involve you. They make you an active participant in a relationship. Questions are the fuel that drives communication.

How to ask her a question

No distractions! Forget about the television and the paper. Do not keep looking at your watch. Stop checking your blackberry or e-mail. Look her in the eye and pay attention. Let her know you are "logged-in" to her.

Link the question to something specific (What would you like to do this weekend? or What did you do today?)

Just listen; this is not the time to evaluate or solve problems.

Assure her you are listening, make noises, "ah hah" or "oh" and "aah".

Smile or laugh at something she says.

Practice listening and asking questions. One great way to do this is to "parrot" back what she said to you. Listen to what she said and repeat what you heard. This will prove to her that you are listening. It will also give her the opportunity to clarify anything that is unclear.

RESPONDING TO YOUR MATE

Learning how to communicate with your wife is the key to success. It unlocks the bedroom door. Words excite women! This is why women talk so much. When your wife stops talking to you, watch out! It is a sure sign that she does not want to be with you anymore.

Your wife may want more attention from you. Some of these complaints may sound familiar:

- "I always do everything around the house!"

- "You never listen to me"

- "Everyone is having more sex than we are!"

- "Are you sure you like my haircut?"

Most women have difficulty asking for love in a way men can act on.

- "Hey baby. I need some sex in an hour. Are you available?"

Do not be defensive or offended! Using words like always, never or every is a key indicator that it is time to listen. This is your wife's way of telling you she is hungry for your attention. This is your clue to feed her!

Women feel you should know what they need and happily give it. The truth is none of us are mind readers. Ask her what she needs and listen to what she says. Give her the attention she needs and happiness awaits both of you.

Happy couples share thoughts, feelings, hopes, dreams, hurt, anger, and longing. They talk and listen to each other. As a result, these couples share a bond. They are each others best friend.

This is your wife and the way she feels love. Follow the menu and watch it work like magic.

CHECKLIST
WHAT HAVE YOU DONE
FOR YOUR MARRIAGE TODAY?

- Have you asked your wife about her day and listened to her answer?

- Have you sincerely complimented her?

- Have you told her you love her?

- Have you hugged and kissed her?

- Have you asked or just done something to help her with the kids or the house?

- Have you done or bought something special just because you love her?

About the Authors

BJ and Laurie Woodard have been happily married for ten years. They are living their dream overlooking the water in Lago Vista, Texas. Together these lovers, friends and confidants share tried-and-true techniques to help you get more out of your own marriage and live a richer, more abundant life!

Laurie Woodard has a degree in Psychology from the University of Michigan. Laurie and BJ have both studied personal development for the past 10 years and have made a lifetime commitment to it.

www.the marriagemanual.com